JUSTIN BIEBER
UNLEASHED

UNAUTHORIZED

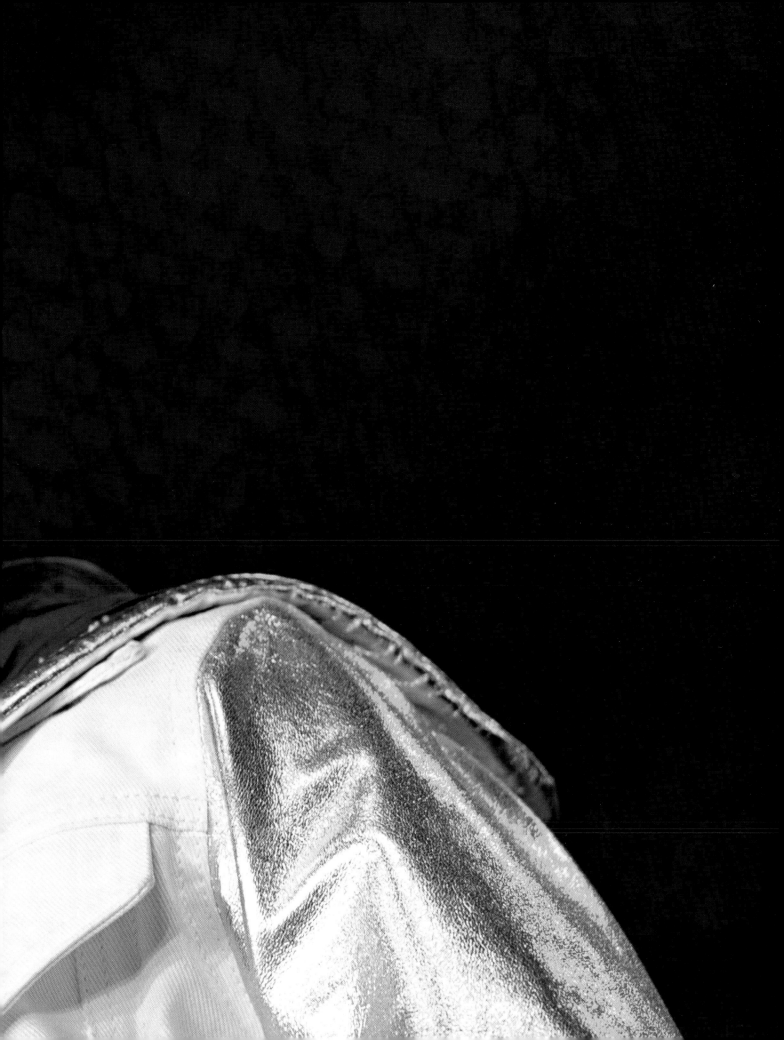

Written by Elise Munier
Edited by Elizabeth Scoggins
Designed by Angie Allison

Picture Acknowledgements:

Michael Buckner/WireImage/Getty Images:
 front cover image, page 6;
Mike Marsland/WireImage/Getty Images:
 back cover image, page 29;
Peter Wafzig/Getty Images: pages 2—3, 9, 43, 62—63;
Ian West/PA Wire/Press Association Images: page 8;
Theo Kingma/Rex Features: pages 10, 15 (left and right);
Dominique Charriau/WireImage/Getty Images: page 11;
Frazer Harrison/Getty Images: page 12 (left);
Chris McGrath/Getty Images: page 12 (centre);
Matt Baron/BEI/Rex Features: page 12 (right);
Picture Perfect/Rex Features: page 13 (left);
Vince Flores/UK Press/Press Association Images:
 page 13 (centre);
Robert Pitts/LANDOV/Press Association Images:
 page 13 (right);
Irving Shuter/Getty Images: page 14;
Broadimage/Rex Features: page 16;
Ian Gavan/Getty Images: pages 19, 24, 44;
Christopher Polk/VF11/Getty Images for Vanity: page 20;
Rob Verhorst/Getty Images: page 25;

Chris McKay/WireImage/Getty Images: page 30;
Jason Merritt/Getty Images: pages 32—33;
Most Wanted/Rex Features: page 35;
Scott Gries/PictureGroup/EMPICS Entertainment/
 Press Association Images: pages 36 and 37;
Francois Durand/Getty Images: page 38 (left);
Stuart Wilson/Getty Images: page 38 (right);
Dave Hogan/Getty Images: page 39;
Kevin Winter/Getty Images: page 48;
Wong Maye-E/AP/Press Association Images/
 Press Association Images: page 51;
Sipa Press/Rex Features: page 54;
Michael Tullberg/Getty Images: page 57 (centre);
KPA/Zuma/Rex Features: page 58;
Jack Guez/AFP/Getty Images: page 59;
Agencia EFE/Rex Features: page 60;
ShutterStock Inc: images on pages 56, 57 (left and right),
58 (left); background graphics on pages 4, 5, 6—7, 10—11,
12—13, 14—15, 16—17, 18, 21, 24—25, 26—27, 28—29, 30—31, 34—35,
36—37, 38—39, 40—41, 42—43, 44—45, 46—47, 48—49, 50—51,
52—53, 54—55, 56—57, 58—59, 60—61.

Published in Great Britain in 2011 by Buster Books,
an imprint of Michael O'Mara Books Limited,
9 Lion Yard, Tremadoc Road, London SW4 7NQ
www.mombooks.com/busterbooks

This edition published in 2011 by
Scholastic Canada Ltd.
604 King Street West, Toronto, Ontario M5V 1E1

Library and Archives Canada Cataloguing in Publication
Munier, Elise
Justin Bieber : unleashed / Elise Munier.
ISBN 978-1-4431-1315-1
1. Bieber, Justin, 1994- --Juvenile literature. 2. Singers--Canada-- Biography--Juvenile literature. I. Title.
ML3930.B545M96 2011   j782.42164092   C2011-903569-3

PLEASE NOTE: This book is not affiliated with or endorsed by Justin Bieber or any of his publishers or licensees.

6 5 4 3 2 1   Printed in Canada 118   11 12 13 14 15

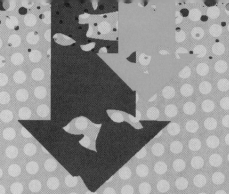

JUSTIN BIEBER
UNLEASHED

UNAUTHORIZED

Scholastic Canada Ltd.
Toronto New York London Auckland Sydney
Mexico City New Delhi Hong Kong Buenos Aires

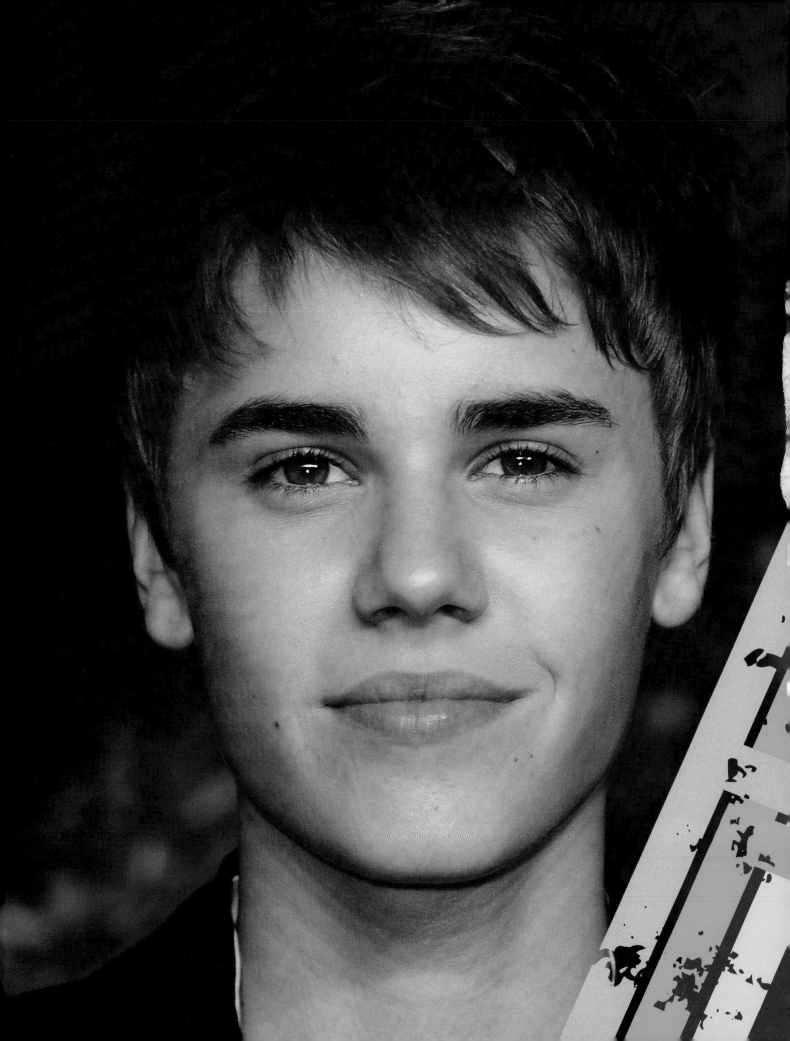

CONTENTS

Welcome to Justin's world! 8

All things Bieber 10

Never say … 12

Growing up 14

And the winner is 16

My words 18

Love me 20

Hair he is! 24

World wide 26

Mad about Justin? 28

A day in the life 30

Guess who! 34

Just the facts 36

Behind the music 38

What kind of fan are you? 40

In the spotlight 42

Biebs in 3D 44

Road to the red carpet 46

Fan-tastic! 48

Tell me 50

Would you rather? 52

Bieber's birthday bash 54

The ultimate fan quiz 56

Born to be somebody 58

All the answers 61

WELCOME TO JUSTIN'S WORLD!

Bieber Fever has swept the world, reaching millions of fabulous fans like you. With your help, Justin has gone from class clown to world-famous pop star in the blink of an eye!

A Shooting Star

Justin Bieber has always loved to sing, but his journey to stardom began when he was just 12 years old. Justin would sing around the house all the time, and he decided to enter a local competition, where he won third prize.

The Biebs didn't stop there — he also uploaded videos of himself singing to YouTube. Seven months and 10 million hits later, Scooter Braun, a managing executive from So So Def Recordings flew Justin and his mother to his offices in Atlanta. Not long after that, in October 2008, Justin signed a record deal with Island Records. The rest is history.

On his journey from small-town boy to international star, Justin has performed on stages all over the world. He's even starred in a documentary film about his life — *Justin Bieber: Never Say Never* — shown all over the world. His albums have sold millions of copies to adoring fans, and his tickets are quickly snatched up, making for tons of sold-out concerts.

What's next for this superstar? His life just keeps getting bigger and better, and this is only the beginning for J-Biebs.

Backstage Pass

This book is your VIP ticket to discovering the amazing world of the planet's hottest singer.

Not only can you get the inside scoop on his life before everyone knew his name (and copied his hairstyle), but you'll see how Justin's adjusting to life in the spotlight as one of the world's biggest stars. Read all about his most-recent superstar successes.

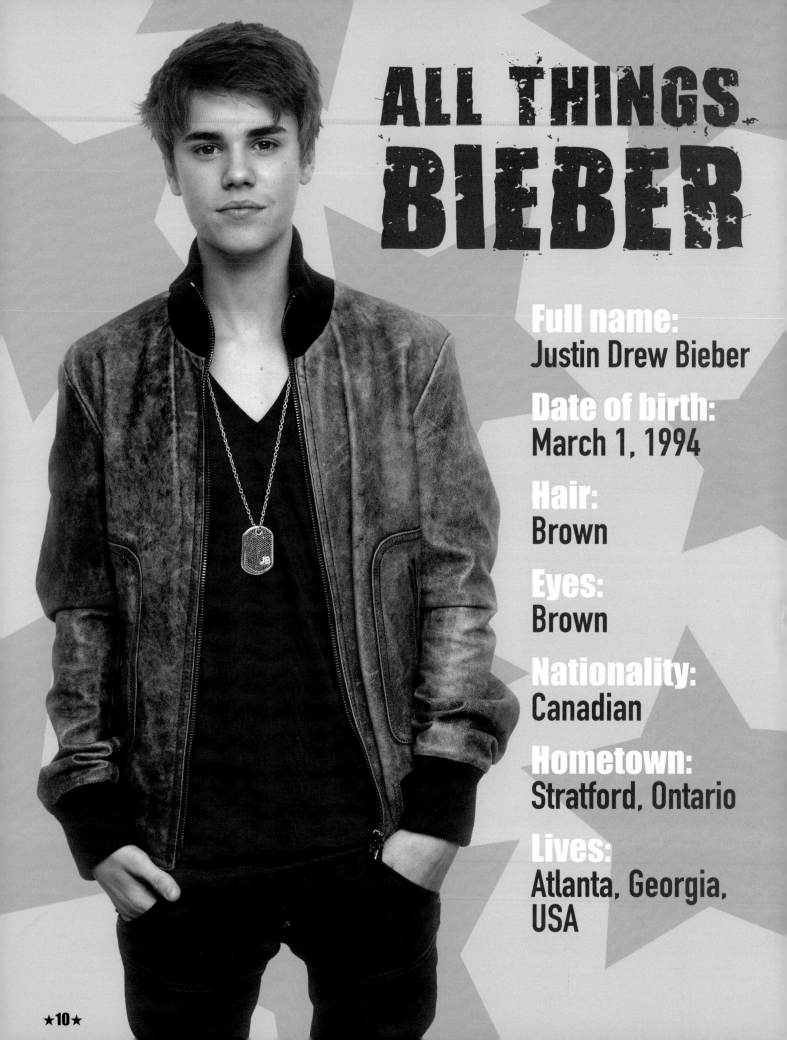

ALL THINGS BIEBER

Full name:
Justin Drew Bieber

Date of birth:
March 1, 1994

Hair:
Brown

Eyes:
Brown

Nationality:
Canadian

Hometown:
Stratford, Ontario

Lives:
Atlanta, Georgia, USA

Fave colour:
Purple

Fave foods:
Spaghetti bolognese, cheesecake and "Big Foot" candy

Fave beverage:
Orange juice

Nicknames:
J–Biebs, JB, Biebs

Fave number:
6

Shoe size:
7 $^1/_2$

Idol:
Wayne Gretzky

Super-power wish:
To fly

Fave sports to play:
Soccer, basketball and hockey

Dream job:
Architect

Grade point average:
4.0

Pets:
A papillon dog called Sam

Funniest TV show:
The Inbetweeners

Hidden talents:
Can solve a Rubik's Cube in under a minute

Pet peeves:
When girls try to impress him, being asked his favourite colour and being cold

Inspirations:
Grandpa and Usher

On his iPod:
Something new and interesting, from Tupac to Tragically Hip

Fave music video:
"Thriller" by Michael Jackson

Likes:
Apple pie

Really likes:
Girls

Dislikes:
Getting up in the morning

Fave coffee chain:
Tim Hortons

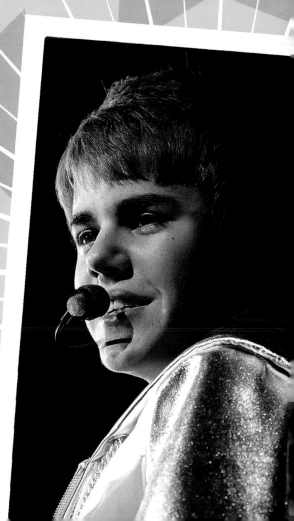

NEVER SAY ...

You might hang on his every word, but can you tell which Tweets are Justin's and who the others belong to? (There are some clues in the pictures below.) Check out page 61 for the answers.

1 Music is the universal language no matter the country we are born in or the color of our skin. Brings us all together

2 Last night was the end of my first tour! I couldn't have had a better time and I owe it all to you guys! Thank You!!! <3

3 Why do u drive on a parkway and park in the driveway. Its messed up

4 its about that time... RANDOM CHUCK NORRIS MOMENT: # Chuck Norris does not style his hair. It lays perfectly in place out of sheer terror.

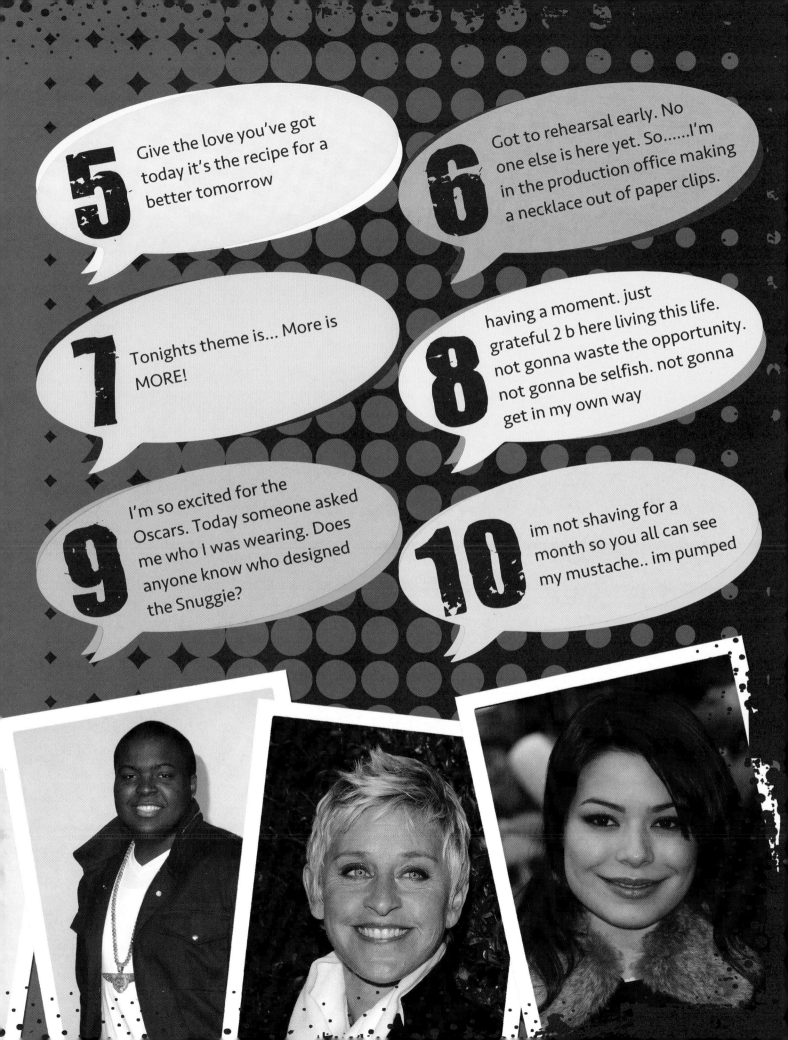

Justin wasn't always standing in the spotlight and roaming the red carpet. Find out what it was like for the Biebs when he was growing up in Stratford, Ontario. From fishing trips to Christmas dinners and everything in between, get the scoop.

grandparents, grandchildren, stepgrandchildren, kids and stepkids — everyone was invited. Then everyone would settle down and eat a delicious turkey and gravy dinner. "I'm telling you," says Justin, "my grandma puts up an awesome Christmas dinner." After dinner, the gift-giving began. The whole family plays a game with dice to decide who gets which wrapped surprise. "Then we all open our gifts and end up trading anyway," Justin says.

What a catch

Justin was happy to get to spend time with his grandparents when he was growing up. One of his favourite memories is going fishing with them every summer at Star Lake. They would rent a cabin, and spend quiet mornings casting fishing lines out on the water. "I hope someday I'll be out on Star Lake with my own grandkid, reeling in brown trout and telling stories about how all of us would get together by the fire pit in the evening," he says. Justin's lucky to have reeled in such great grandparents.

Family Feast

Christmases at the Biebers' were a big event! The whole family came, including

Lucky Lad

Justin is truly grateful for his family. "That's how we are in my family. Every person gives what they have," says Justin. The down-to-earth star knows there is no such thing as a normal family, and he's glad his family aren't perfect. "They'd

probably be the most boring people ever. Or the scariest," he grins. Justin loves his family, and no matter how many family issues there may be, he wouldn't trade them for the world.

Meet the Parents

Bieber admires his parents — especially his mom for being a single mother, and being able to work and raise him, "a little prankster," as he calls himself. Definitely a family man, Justin is thankful for everything his parents have given him. "My dad has influenced not only my life but my music," Justin says. Even though his dad worked a lot, Justin loved spending time playing guitar with him and listening to classic rock.

Don't Mess with the Biebs

It seems unbelievable that anyone would pick on him now, but when Justin was in middle school, he was pretty short — even most of the girls were taller than he was! But Justin defended himself against bullies, mostly resolving things peacefully. One time Justin got sucked into a huge fight at school. "I was never a big fighter," Justin says. "I preferred to compete on the basketball court or slice and dice them with my hockey skills." He might prefer peace, but don't mess with this superstar! He says, "I'm not a fighter by nature, but if I believe in something, I stand up for it."

Class Clown

If Justin got in trouble for anything at school, it was usually for clowning around. He would play around on his skateboard, stir things up with his buddies or make someone laugh. But he never really got in trouble for being mean at school. "Basically, I got in trouble for being myself, and that didn't seem fair to me," says the Biebs.

AND THE WINNER IS

Justin may be only 17 years old, but he's already been nominated for and accepted several major music awards. He's lost some and won some, but there are definitely many more awards coming in the music star's bright future. Find out about the awards Justin has snatched up, and which ones he just missed.

Stratford Idol

In September 2007, Justin competed in a local talent competition in his hometown of Stratford, Ontario. He was just 12 years old, and had never been trained by a vocal coach like most of his fellow competitors. Still, Justin was able to win third place! "I thought it would be a fun prize," he admitted, "but I was more into the idea of getting up in front of people and doing music just to see how it felt." He admits that he was a bit crushed not to win at the time, but that he's glad for the way things worked out.

Gaga at the Grammies

In January 2010, Justin presented an award at the 52nd Annual Grammy Awards — along with fellow new artist Ke$ha. But at the 2011 Grammy Awards, Justin was nominated for not just one of the prestigious awards, but two! He says, "All my life I have wanted to win a Grammy."

Justin was nominated for Best New Artist and Best Pop Vocal Album, along with other superstars including Lady Gaga and Katy Perry. Unfortunately, Bieber lost out to Lady Gaga for Best Pop Vocal Album and to Best New Artist winner Esperanza Spalding.

Even though the Biebs didn't sweep up any trophies this time, Esperanza Spalding says, "He [Justin] was very gracious, and we met right after the show and exchanged hair touches. He was very sweet and gracious and he didn't seem upset. Very kind young man."

The Junos

At the Juno music awards in 2010, Justin was nominated for New Artist of the Year, but he lost out to hip-hop star Drake. Justin wasn't giving up that easily though!

In 2011, he was nominated for a whopping four Juno Awards and he took home the prize for Pop Album of the Year for *My World 2.0* and Fan Choice Award — the only category voted for by the public.

MuchMusic Awards

At the MuchMusic Awards, which Miley Cyrus hosted in 2010, out of four nominations Justin snagged both UR Fave New Artist and UR Fave Canadian Video. But he had two songs in the category of International Video of the Year by a Canadian, so JB beat himself when he won for "One Time." You can't win them all!

All That Glitters ...

Justin is grateful for his success and loves to be nominated for awards. But he knows that awards and prizes aren't everything. "Usher reminds me on a regular basis that there will be a whole lot of awards given out during the course of my career," he says. "It's an honour to be nominated and awesome to win, but you can't lose sight of the real honours and victories that happen off camera."

MY WORDS

Get ready to do some serious searching! Ten words connected with Justin and his superstar world are hidden in the grid below and it's your job to find them. They could be going forwards, backwards, up, down or even diagonally. Check your answers on page 61.

Z	Y	G	O	S	O	S	B	F	G	J	Y	U	D	P
E	M	C	F	E	T	E	E	M	J	É	S	S	B	L
U	M	C	I	Q	Y	R	L	L	Q	L	J	M	Y	F
S	A	G	Y	O	S	T	A	P	E	O	X	I	B	H
A	R	P	N	E	J	J	E	T	Y	N	E	L	A	C
T	G	C	D	Z	N	H	L	G	F	G	A	E	B	O
H	É	R	E	T	T	I	W	T	A	O	I	N	J	O
Z	C	G	F	É	H	O	Q	B	L	Z	R	P	C	W
Q	S	D	Z	O	I	O	H	S	L	P	R	D	I	Q
L	Q	H	V	B	N	N	O	X	C	A	Z	J	W	V
D	O	P	Z	X	P	H	N	N	Y	O	K	I	H	Y
F	B	W	B	Q	Q	T	U	F	P	B	O	R	W	D
Z	H	Z	J	R	E	L	L	I	R	H	T	T	É	M
I	U	T	L	Q	I	W	F	F	F	O	H	T	E	M
Q	T	L	J	C	G	P	H	M	Q	Y	X	U	O	R

BABY

BEYONCÉ

GRAMMY
THRILLER

PRAY
TWITTER

SCOOTER
U SMILE

SELENA

STRATFORD

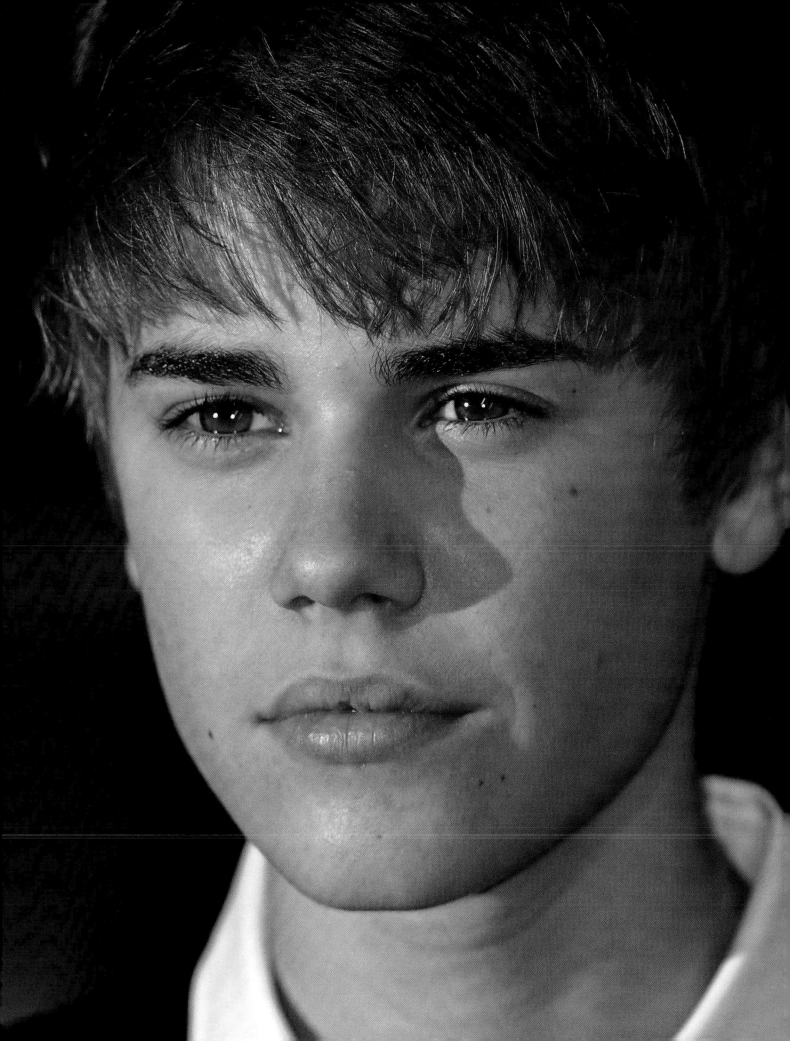

LOVE ME

Justin's cute smile and sweet songs go straight to the hearts of his adoring fans. But what about Justin and love? Get up-close-and-personal with the Biebs right here, and find out all about what goes on in his heart.

Ladies' Man

"I really like girls ... girls ... girls ... girls ... girls ... girls ... girls," grins Justin. He's clearly a fan of the ladies, but what kind of girl is he looking for? As far as looks go, he admits that "pretty eyes and a nice smile" are sure to turn his head. But that's not the most important thing for him. With his crazy, superstar lifestyle, the Biebs needs to be able to be a regular 17-year-old guy sometimes, so his favourite girl needs to be down-to-earth. Justin's also a legendary prankster, so a good sense of humour and the ability to make him laugh is a must.

Justin's heart doesn't flutter when girls wear loads of make-up to try and impress him. For him, it's all about letting natural beauty shine through. What's more, you don't have to be super-famous to win his heart. "I would definitely date a fan," says Justin with a smile. "It would depend on the circumstances, but I don't rule out anybody."

Love for the Fab Fans

Justin's worldwide army of devoted Biebettes are some of the most important people in his life. Every one of his fans is special to him, and Justin loves performing so he can connect with them. "One of my favourite moments in every show is when I get to walk downstage, look right into those beautiful eyes and tell you, 'If you need me, I'll come running from a thousand miles away ...'" he says. In 2011, he even decided to make each of his fans his Valentine on February 14th. Wow, what a heart-throb!

Dream Guy

If Justin picked you to be his date, you're sure to be one less lonely girl. Justin says his ideal night out would be to get something to eat, chat, and really get to know a girl. "I hate being on a date where both people are working too hard to come up with stuff to say," he says. "You know it's working when you can just chill — listen to music, watch a movie or whatever — without feeling like you have to force the conversation. It should just be natural."

After the first date's gone well, you can bet he'd make a wonderful boyfriend. At the Vanity Fair Oscars Party in 2011, Justin took to the red carpet with Disney starlet Selena Gomez. She looked beautiful in a long scarlet dress, and Justin had sweetly made sure his outfit matched his date's perfectly. He was looking super-suave in a tux, with a bright red handkerchief poking out of his jacket pocket.

So he's got attention to detail down, but what about some good old-fashioned romance? Justin was reportedly so smitten with Selena that he sent her enough bouquets of flowers to fill her house while he was away on tour. Awww!

Young at Heart

Justin says he's having a great time dating, and hanging out with girls, but he's definitely not ready to settle down yet. "I think love is a learning process throughout your life," he says. "I'm still learning, I'm still trying to figure out girls!"

HAIR HE IS!

It's the look that gripped the world like extra-hold hairspray — the Justin Bieber hairstyle. Read on to find out all about those luscious locks.

Fantastic Flip

It wasn't just the original hair-do itself that caught fans' attention. Justin also had his adorable signature "flip." But why does he do it? Justin admits that he flips his sleek bangs out of his face with a simple head shake because his hair gets out of place. It must help him to see out from under all that hair, too!

More than Just a Haircut

Also known as the Twitch, Flip, Switch or Flow, the Bieber look became the hottest boy-style around. But surely it must have taken hours for JB to get his hair always looking so perfect? The Biebs confessed — "After I shower," he says, "I blow dry my hair and just shake it and it goes like that." That's hair-raisingly amazing!

Get the Look

Justin's trademark floppy locks have been a magnet for girls. The haircut must be really magical, as some boys have paid up to $175 to get the Bieber-look.

Trimming the Tresses

Early in 2011, Justin told MTV that he was thinking about cutting his hair a bit shorter after the premiere of his film *Never Say Never*. But no one predicted the mass hysteria that trimming the star's signature hair-do caused. Bieber's hairstylist, Vanessa Price, calls it the "Justin Bieber 2011," but some fans have not quite adjusted to his new look. Nearly 80,000 of his fans were so upset, they stopped following him on Twitter!

Shortly after he chopped off his cool coif, Justin tweeted about it. "yeah so it's true…i got a lil haircut…i like it…and we are giving all the hair cut to CHARITY to auction. Details coming soon…" The supersweet singer gave a lock of his hair to TV show host Ellen DeGeneres, who auctioned off the sacred strands for $40,668 after 98 bids. All the money will go to The Gentle Barn Foundation, an animal rescue organization.

WORLD WIDE

Toronto, Ontario, Canada
In February 2011, Justin's film *Never Say Never* premiered on home ground in Toronto — JB even held his own press conference, inviting a group of fans to watch. "What's the point if my fans aren't in here, right?" he asked sweetly.

Los Angeles, California, USA
Justin took time out from touring to take part in an NBA All-Star Celebrity game. Despite being beaten 54–49, Justin still clinched the title of most valuable player — proving he's a huge hit on stage *and* on the basketball court.

Miami, Florida, USA
In exchange for a donation to the relief effort in Japan, following the earthquake and tsunami there, true Beliebers can pose for photos with a genuine lock of Justin's hair. The trimmed tresses, on display at a bowling alley, were recovered from his February haircut — the hair even has its own security guards!

New York, New York, USA
Back in August 2010, JB took to the stage at the world-famous venue Madison Square Garden — that concert had sold out in just 22 minutes and footage from his performance became the fabulous finale of *Never Say Never*.

Justin has been all over the world — from Japan to Australia, and Germany to the USA. His My World Tour — his first headlining tour — hit eighty-five cities in the USA and Canada, where he performed for nearly two million fans. He's been to loads of cities, but here's the scoop on some that he's been to and what happened while he was on the road.

Liverpool, UK

In March 2011, fans hoping to catch a glimpse of the Biebs made so much noise outside his hotel that fifty police officers had to hold them back. Justin even sent out a plea for quiet on his Twitter feed, so he could go to sleep.

Manchester, UK

Justin couldn't resist playing the pranking older brother when Willow Smith joined him on his UK tour — during one performance of "Whip My Hair" in March, little Willow was startled when JB and her older brother, Jaden, leaped on stage and started dancing with her. She didn't let them put her off though, and introduced them as her new back-up dancers.

Paris, France

In February 2011, police had to shut a shop when fans mobbed the Biebs at a meet-and-greet.

Tokyo, Japan

Justin stuck to his commitment to complete his tour in Japan, despite a few safety concerns following the earthquake and tsunami there earlier in the year. In May 2011, he finished things off with a spectacular concert in Japan's capital city, announcing on Twitter that he would donate some of the proceeds to the Japanese Red Cross.

Kuala Lumpur, Malaysia

Fans were so excited about Justin's forthcoming concert in April 2011 that they organized a flashmob, dancing brilliantly to a mash-up of the Biebs' hits.

Sydney, Australia

At a concert in the city in May 2011, someone threw eggs at the stage, luckily missing the Biebs. But the next day, Justin did have a little egg on his face after disrupting take-off by wandering around. JB apologized to flight attendants and buckled up.

MAD ABOUT JUSTIN?

Justin's the perfect prince of pop — you're his number one fan, but what would you say to him?

Fill in the lines below by following the instructions or using one of the choices in brackets.

I'm mad about Justin Bieber! He is the most _Cutest_ singer in the entire world. I think that he is so cool because of the way he _he wear's his hats and his dance moves_ (helps others, sings & dances, jokes around) and the purple _hoodie_ (hat, shoes, hoodie) he wears. _Purple_ is my favourite colour. (Your favourite colour)

The coolest thing about Justin is his _hat's_, and I just love his sweet _smile and songs._ (songs, smile, dance moves). Nobody can sing like Bieber can!

His best song is _Never say_ _Never_ (your favourite song), and my favourite music video is _Somebody to love_ ♡ (your favourite video).

If I could meet him, I would tell him that I'm his number one fan because I know _1000_ (number) of his songs by heart, and I think he is the best. I would really like to eat ~~popcorn~~ _pasta_ (your fave meal) at my fave restaurant, and then we could go to _Wonderland_ (a place you love to go) together.

Justin is my idol because _he wants to make a difference in the world._

One day, I hope I get the chance to meet him. Justin, I _LOVE_ (verb) you!

A DAY IN THE LIFE

You can only imagine what a typical day is like for the Biebs. Read on to get the scoop on all the things Justin does in a day.

A Typical Day

Aside from the normal stuff everyone does, such as wake up, shower, brush his teeth and eat, a normal day for Justin Bieber is definitely not your average twenty-four hours. "Every day is different," says Justin. He could be doing anything — from interviews, to performing or even going on a photoshoot. But one thing is for sure, many typical days for the Biebs are long ones. "I have a lot of people who want to talk to me," he says, "and I am doing a lot of TV shows and stuff."

One thing Justin is sure to do every day is practise his dance moves, and do some vocal exercises. "The voice is like any other muscle. You have to exercise it," he reveals. Justin admits that it can all be a bit much, and sometimes he needs to take a breath. He says that he normally gets only about six hours of sleep a night, but he definitely enjoys what he's doing.

Life in the Spotlight

What's a day like for the Biebs when he's performing? Read on to find out what one New York morning show performance was like for Justin in the summer of 2010.

Justin wakes up early — while it's still dark — to make it to the show by 6:15 a.m. Next, he does some vocal warm-ups at the show's studio, and then goes for a TV interview before his performance. After the interview, Justin takes the stage in front of a crowd of fans. Some of them have been waiting since the night before to see him. After the performance, there's still a photoshoot, filming of another TV performance and even school work to do. Justin Bieber is so grateful to be doing what he loves, and it may seem like a glamorous life, but it can also be exhausting!

GUESS WHO!

Which is false, which is true? See if you know!

Everyone knows that Justin has a heart of gold and he's done some pretty amazing things for charities. Read on to see if you can decide which acts of kindness were performed by the Biebs and which were not. Then check out page 61 for the answers.

1. For Justin's birthday, he asked his fans to help him raise $5,000 to help provide wells for people who do not have access to clean water.

2. Justin auctioned off a space suit for charity.

3. In August 2010, Justin raised over $32,690 by donating $1.06 from each ticket he sold for his concert in Nashville, Tennessee, USA.

4. Justin signed a wooden dog bone to be auctioned off to raise money for the Mississippi Animal Rescue League.

5. During his career, Justin has helped to form the ONE Campaign — a charity that helps people who have AIDS and those who live in poverty.

6. Justin performed and helped answer phones at a telethon in 2010 to help raise money for the earthquake victims of Haiti, along with other superstars like Mary J. Blige and Akon.

7. Justin donated a handwritten copy of his book to help raise money for the charity Book Aid International — a charity that shares books with those who can't afford them.

8. In 2010, Justin gave bedside concerts to patients at a hospital in New York. "This is what really matters," he said about his visit.

9. Justin helped to raise money for a charity called Pencils of Promise, which helps to give an education to kids around the world.

10. Recently, Justin decorated a yoga bag to auction off for the benefit of a breast cancer charity.

JUST THE FACTS

If you want to be a true Belieber, you've got to know the facts! Find out everything there is to know about Justin — from what he loves to his best friends' names and so much more.

Did You Know?

JB loves going to the movies and playing video games.

Quoi? Did you say Justin is bilingual? He can speak English and French!

His worst habit is eating too much candy.

He got to throw the first pitch at a baseball game in Chicago, in 2010.

Justin's best friends' names are Christian and Ryan.

In February 2010, a false rumour was spread about Justin that he had died!

Bieber taught himself to play the guitar, piano, trumpet and drums.

Justin has a younger half-brother and half-sister, whose names are Jaxon and Jazmyn.

The Biebs like to draw.

One of his ambitions is to perform a duet with music star Beyoncé.

Justin prefers white bread over brown.

Justin's fave superhero is Superman.

He hates Ugg boots on girls.

He doesn't get nervous when performing in front of thousands of people.

Justin is a daredevil. He even bungee jumped off a bridge while he was in New Zealand.

The Biebs doesn't own a wallet. He just stuffs things in his pockets.

Justin secretly loves the film The Notebook.

His hobbies include playing sports, skateboarding and breakdancing.

His fave breakfast food is Cap'n Crunch cereal.

Justin Timberlake offered to sign Bieber, but Usher won Justin's heart in the end.

JB loves golf.

Justin has a tattoo of a bird in flight on his hip. It's a family tradition, and his dad has one, too.

The Biebs is left-handed.

When Justin was born, singer Celine Dion's "The Power of Love" was number one on the Billboard charts.

Justin's mom travels with him when he's on the road.

Justin doesn't know the US National Anthem, but can sing the Canadian one in both languages!

The name of Justin's vocal coach is Jan Smith, but he sometimes calls her Mama Jan.

JB had his first kiss at age 13.

His fave TV show is Smallville and his fave movie is Rocky IV.

JB's fave hockey team is the Toronto Maple Leafs.

JB has both of his ears pierced.

BEHIND THE MUSIC

You know all the words to every Justin Bieber song. You've got the moves from every video down pat. But do you know the story behind each song? Get the backstage lowdown.

One Time

In the video for the hit song "One Time," Justin takes over Usher's house and throws a fabulous party. Justin got to fly his best friend, Ryan, in to Atlanta so he could be in the video, and Usher even helped out with the production. They all had a blast making the video, and planned on releasing it a few weeks after the single came out. But that's not how it happened!

Somehow, the video got posted on iTunes two weeks before it was supposed to be there! Scooter, Justin's manager (pictured below), was steaming mad at first because the song was there early and no one knew about it. So Justin posted the news on Facebook and Twitter.

A few days later, "One Time" was the number three song on the iTunes chart.

Down to Earth

Justin wrote the song "Down to Earth" for his first album, *My World*. He was really excited about it, and it's become a huge fan favourite. Justin likes the song because people can really connect with the emotional lyrics.

Usher told Justin that some songs work best when the singer can really show his true feelings. Justin thinks that this song lets his

deep feelings shine through. Bieber also loves that this song "doesn't need any spectacular stage effects in the touring show; the best thing I can do is just sing it straight from my heart." He admits, "Sometimes the emotion of it is enough to bring tears to my eyes."

One Less Lonely Girl

The video for "One Less Lonely Girl" has been called "the musical equivalent of a chick flick." People have also said it was corny, but Justin disagrees — and so do thousands of fans! In the video, the gorgeous girl who is cast opposite Justin drops a scarf while she's at the laundromat. Justin then sends her on a truly sweet treasure hunt — complete with sweet notes, PUPPIES and flowers — to get it back.

"I didn't immediately get that they meant it as an insult," admits Justin. "They dissed this part where there are some puppies at a pet shop, and I was like 'What? Who doesn't like puppies? And more important, who thinks pretending not to like puppies will make them more attractive to girls?'"

Baby

This video, which was shot in a bowling alley, was inspired by one of Justin's musical heroes, Michael Jackson. "We're kind of going off the 'You Make Me Feel' video ... I'm following her around trying to get the girl," he reveals. And Justin really was chasing the girl! When his beautiful co-star, Jasmine Villegas, asked him why he was chasing her around the bowling alley, he answered, "Because you are just so gorgeous and you have such a stunning personality."

Not only does Justin know how to charm the ladies, but he also has some sweet moves on the dance floor. In the video, Justin got to show off his moon-walking skills — one of Michael Jackson's signature moves.

WHAT KIND OF FAN ARE YOU?

START HERE
OMG! The Biebs is having a concert in your town. What do you do?

Raid your wardrobe for the perfect concert-going gear.

Your fave outfit has a stain on it. What do you do?

Call your BFFs and find the perfect accessory to cover up the damage.

Check out some music videos for inspiration and head to the mall.

Design an eye-catching poster to take to the show.

Your poster looks really blah. What do you do?

Hit the shops so you can glam it up with glitter-glue.

Add some fab photos of you and the Biebs.

The outfit looks better, but not great. What do you do?

Shrug it off. You just can't wait to see the show.

Accessorize until the stain is undetectable!

Justin's Manager
You could be Justin's manager. You are cool, calm and collected, yet stylish and fun.

Bieber Stylist
You love all things Bieber, especially his super-cute hair and his stunning outfits. In addition to a fab fan, you'd make a superb stylist.

Justin is spotted shopping at the store you are in. What do you do?

Nearly faint. His outfit is even cooler in person than you ever imagined.

Start singing your fave Bieber song at the top of your voice.

Singing Star
You know all the lyrics and every tune there is. You love Justin, but you absolutely adore his music.

Making sure that you and your friends know all the words to all the songs.

It's just minutes to showtime. What are you doing?

Dancin' Diva!
You've got all the moves, and you just love the way Justin dances. You're a dreamer just waiting to dance your way to the spotlight one day.

Practising all the moves from Justin's latest video.

IN THE SPOTLIGHT

It's been quite a journey for Justin, from his very first hit single, to tours across the world and film premieres. Check out some of his biggest moments in the spotlight.

March 1, 1994: Little Biebs appears on the scene — born in London, Ontario.

September 2007: Justin wins third place in the Stratford Idol competition.

October 2008: Justin is officially signed to Island Records.

July 7, 2009: Bieber's first single, "One Time," hits radio airwaves in the USA.

November 17, 2009: *My World*, Justin's debut album is released.

December 22, 2009: *My World* sells over one million copies, and Justin is awarded a platinum album disc.

March 23, 2010: Justin's second album, *My World 2.0*, tops the US charts.

March 28, 2010: The premiere of Justin's TV show, *The Diary of Justin Bieber*, airs on MTV, to give fans a behind-the-scenes peek into his life.

April 5, 2010: Justin performs at The White House Easter Egg Roll — an Easter celebration concert.

June 23, 2010: Justin's first headline tour — visiting towns and cities around North America — kicks off in Hartford, Connecticut.

October 12, 2010: *Justin Bieber: First Step 2 Forever: My Story*, Justin's memoir, is released.

November 19, 2010: *My World 2.0* has sold over 2 million copies. Justin is awarded a double platinum disc.

December 2, 2010: Justin is nominated for two Grammy Awards.

December 23, 2010: The *My World* tour ends in Atlanta, Georgia.

February 8, 2011: Hundreds of fans come out to see Justin and his film, *Never Say Never*, in 3D at the Los Angeles film premiere.

February 13, 2011: Justin hits the red carpet at the Grammys in style. Even though he doesn't win, he's still shining bright.

February 21, 2011: Justin cuts his gorgeous trademark hair! But it doesn't stop him looking super-cute.

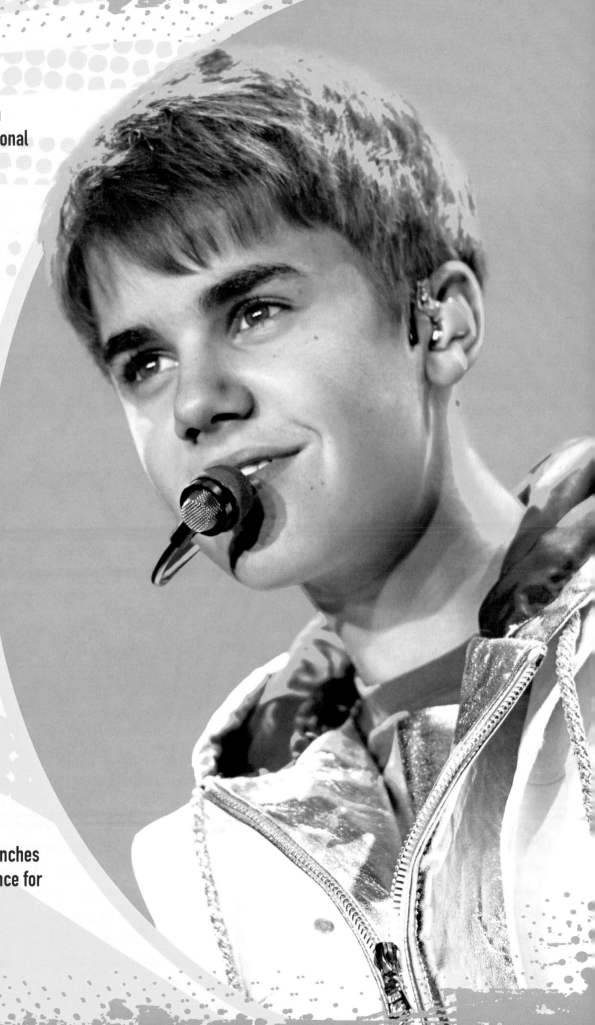

March 4, 2011: Justin kicks off his international *My World* tour in Birmingham, UK.

March 25, 2011: Justin contributes his song "Pray" to *Songs for Japan*, a charity album released today to raise money following the earthquake and tsunami.

March 27, 2011: It's a double win for Justin at the Juno Awards — Pop Album of the Year for *My World 2.0* and the Fan Choice Award.

May 22, 2011: Out of a phenomenal 11 nominations, Justin storms home with 6 Billboard Awards!

June 2011: Justin launches his own floral fragrance for girls, Someday.

BIEBS IN 3D

You've seen him on stage, on countless TV shows and in tons of newspapers and magazines, but this year, Justin Bieber has made it to the big screen in his very own 3D film.

Hollywood Buzz

On August 2, 2010, not long after he'd told the world he was releasing a memoir, Justin stopped hearts all over the world when he broke the news — he would be starring in his own 3D film all about his rise to fame. The film, which was directed by John M. Chu, was released to the public on February 11, 2011, just in time for Valentine's Day.

Fan Power

Thanks to devoted fans like you, the film, which sees Justin go from small town nobody to filling Madison Square Garden, is already one of the bestselling documentaries of all time. Director John M. Chu admitted that Bieber has such a strong group of fans, he was afraid he might mess up the movie for them.

Reach for the Stars

The Biebs believes that the film has something for everyone, and hopes that it will inspire people, saying "If you just focus, and keep your dreams in front of you … and never give up — never say never — then anything is possible."

Fan Phenomenon

Fans couldn't wait to see JB's Hollywood debut. They tweeted, they waited and they rushed to the box office. Justin even encouraged his fans to come out and see his film by spreading the word on Twitter. Hundreds of fans showed Justin their support by going to see the film and tweeting him encouraging messages. And Justin showed his fans how much he loves them by showing up and surprising some of them at movie theatres in the US.

During the Los Angeles premiere, the girls in the audience screamed so loudly, especially during the scenes where Justin was shown performing at concerts, that it felt more like a live performance than a film.

Perfect Premiere

At the film's premiere in Los Angeles, on February 8, 2011, crowds of Beliebers lined the red carpet to wait for the Biebs to arrive. It was also a star-studded event. Usher, Diddy and many others came to support Justin's film debut.

Around the World

Justin didn't have just one premiere, he had quite a few — in Los Angeles, USA; in London, UK; and in Paris, France. Throngs of excited fans joined him on his fabulous nights to catch a glimpse of the Biebs on-screen and off.

Justin was really excited to get to share the experience with his fans. "we flew 13 hours to make the #allstargame but the French Premiere of #NSN3D was crazy...je t'aime —" he tweeted.

The Biebs also wants the film to show his fans that they can reach their goals. "the response around the world to #NEVERSAYNEVER3D is amazing. we want the movie to inspire people to go after their dreams," tweeted Justin.

ROAD TO THE RED CARPET

There's no time to lose! Your career is on the rise, but you'll have to race to make it to the red carpet first.

How to play

Place a counter for each player on "start," grab a die and get going! Take turns to roll the die and move the number of spaces shown, then follow the instructions on the board.

START

Your YouTube video gets a million hits!

Jump forward 3 spaces.

You forgot to do your homework after your concert.

Head to the time-out zone.

Your first single is being played on the radio!

Roll again.

You get signed to a great label!

Jump forward 1 space.

Your first show is sold out!

Jump forward 3 spaces.

YOU WIN!

Everyone's taking your photo on the red carpet.

Roll again.

You've been nominated for a ton of awards.

Move forward 3 spaces

Your album is a huge success!

Roll again.

Uh oh. You need to practise your interview skills.

Miss a turn.

Exhausted from an all-day photoshoot.

Go back 1 space.

Everyone wants your autograph.

Jump forward 1 space.

FAN·

JB has loads of fabulous fans. Find out what they get up to here.

For the Fans

Justin is so grateful to his wonderful fans — that's you! He knows that without you, he'd never have gotten the chance to be where he is now. "My dreams used to be a one-in-a-million chance," he admits. "I never forget that none of this world would have happened without you."

Biebs Medicine

Justin loves to serenade his fans on stage when he's performing in a concert. One night, Justin had one of his lovely fans in the spotlight with him. He sang to her and then handed her his hat.

The next day, this lovely fan started chemotherapy — a special treatment for cancer — and she

TASTIC!

was very scared. She went through lots of tests and struggled with her disease, but she says that looking at the pictures of Justin that decorated her hospital room, remembering the hat he'd given her and chatting with the doctors and nurses about all-things Bieber kept her spirits high. When she lost all her hair as a result of the treatment, the fan wore Justin's hat.

The fan, who is now on her way to a long, healthy life, wrote Justin a terrific thank-you letter. "I'll keep praying for her," Justin says. "So many fans I've met along the road have taught me to never forget to 'Never Say Never.'"

The Sweetest Thing

There are Beliebers of all ages and backgrounds. One of the cutest little Biebettes is Cody, who was just three years old when she fell for Justin. In a YouTube video that was posted in 2010, little Cody is seen crying because she loves Justin and she can't see him. Not long after, Justin appeared on the TV show *Jimmy Kimmel Live!* in Los Angeles, where he met Cody backstage. She was thrilled to see him and gave him a big hug. "Funny thing is," reveals Justin, "I was just as excited to meet her."

You've Got a Friend

Justin's popularity hasn't stopped him remembering how tough things can be for other people. When Casey Heynes, a 15-year-old Australian boy, who has been bullied almost as long as he can remember, stood up to one of his tormentors, he had no idea where it would lead.

The Biebs heard about his story and decided to show Casey some support, bringing him up on stage in Melbourne, Australia, and later tweeting that Casey is "a real life hero." Aww.

TELL ME

Bieber has a lot to say — from Twitter to interviews all over the world. Here are some of the latest and greatest Bieb-tastic quotes.

"My mom is an absolute sweetheart ..."

"What kind of jerk doesn't want love? I bet 95% of sixteen-year-old guys would admit to thinking forty-five girl-related thoughts every three minutes."

"A lot can change in three years ... it's unreal"

"The success I've achieved comes to me from God ..."

"I'm a proud Canadian and I hope that comes through in everything I do"

"No better feeling than coming back home and seeing your grandparents standing there waiting for u. no judgments. pure love"

"My fans are amazing. They will always come to my rescue."

"You have to let yourself do stuff you're not good at"

"One day I noticed the world was full of beautiful girls"

"Music brings people together and that is what I am proudest of"

"I was up in the sky. I was up there among the stars! It was just nuts"

"I want everything to go right. I don't want to let anyone down"

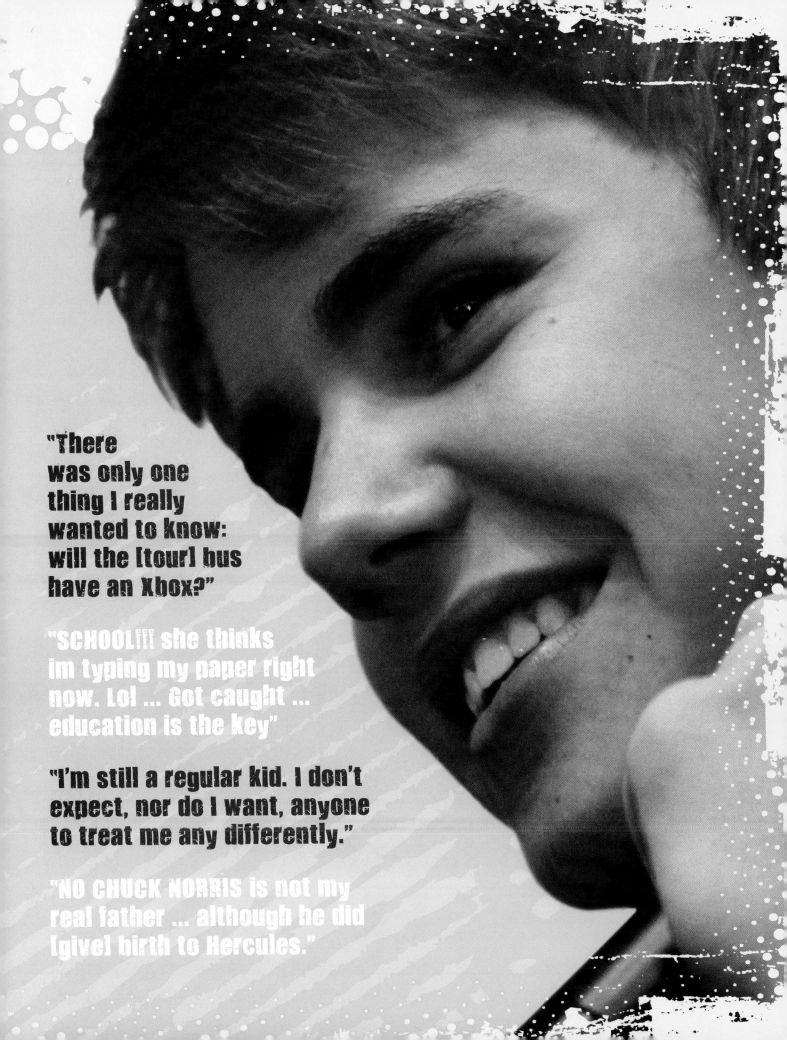

"There was only one thing I really wanted to know: will the [tour] bus have an Xbox?"

"SCHOOL!!! she thinks im typing my paper right now. Lol ... Got caught ... education is the key"

"I'm still a regular kid. I don't expect, nor do I want, anyone to treat me any differently."

"NO CHUCK NORRIS is not my real father ... although he did [give] birth to Hercules."

WOULD YOU RATHER?

If you had the chance to meet Justin Bieber, which of these fab things would you choose?

Go on holiday with Justin
OR
Go on tour with Justin?

Bake him your fave cake
OR
Have Justin cook for you?

Hang out with him
and his friends
OR
Be in his next video?

Write your own song with Justin
OR
Sing "Never Say Never" together
at the top of your lungs?

Head to the skate park
OR
Learn to play guitar
with the Biebs?

Eat ice cream together
OR
Munch popcorn with
him at the cinema?

Sing a song together
OR
Show him your sweet dance moves?

Take photos of you together
OR
Attend a photoshoot with the Biebs?

Be his guest at a film premiere
OR
Walk the red carpet as his competition at the Grammys?

Perform with Justin onstage at a concert
OR
Go to the show with VIP, front row tickets?

Take the Biebs to your fave restaurant
OR
Ride your fave roller coaster together?

Go for a ride in a jet with Justin
OR
Take a spin in a limo with him?

BIEBER'S BIRTHDAY BASH

Hundreds of fans wished Justin a happy birthday, but what did he do for the big 1-7? Read on to find out how the Biebs celebrated his special day.

The Perfect Party

He's the youngest male solo artist to top the Billboard chart since Stevie Wonder did it in 1963. He's stood on the red carpets of many major events, including the world-famous Grammy Awards, and his first record has gone double-platinum. By his 17th birthday, Bieber's debut film, *Never Say Never*, had already earned $60 million at the box office. So what did he do to celebrate his birthday?

Belieb it or not, Justin did not have a huge birthday blowout when he turned 17. Justin had only four days to relax between tours, so he wanted to chill with his grandparents on his special day. Justin reveals, "My grandma makes the best cheesecake — cherry cheesecake. She made that for my 13th birthday." No big party plans meant that Justin was able to celebrate 17 exactly how he wanted to — just relaxing with his family before heading back out on the road. Now that's a perfect party!

Birthday Wishes

His 17th birthday may not have been a major event, but it was a big day for his fans. Hundreds of them posted their wishes for a happy birthday to Justin on Twitter and Facebook. Some even made YouTube videos, which they posted online, to share with their favourite star. Justin tweeted, "thank u ... and ...great bday. flew in grandma and got my cake. hung out with friends. got surprised."

Party Planner

Justin didn't have a big party this year, but what would you have planned to make his 17th birthday the best party ever? Use the space below to share what you would have done.

THE ULTIMATE FAN QUIZ

So you think you know all there is about Justin Bieber? Test your knowledge to find out if you're really the ultimate fan. The answers are on page 61.

1. On Justin's first date, what dish did he spill on his shirt?

a. Pasta carbonara   b. Spaghetti bolognese   c. Pea soup

2. The Biebs' first headlining tour was called:

a. *My World Tour*   b. *My World 2.0 Tour*   c. *Justin Bieber Tour*

3. Which of these stars has Justin not admitted to having a crush on?

a. Kim Kardashian   b. Beyoncé   c. Gwen Stefani

4. Justin was discovered on this popular website:

a. Twitter   b. YouTube   c. Facebook

5. In which city was Justin's hat snatched by excited fans?

a. Auckland, New Zealand   b. New York, USA   c. London, United Kingdom

6. Who is Justin's manager?

a. Usher   b. Jay-Z   c. Scooter Braun

7. How old was Justin when he started playing the drums?

a. 10   b. 6   c. 2

8. Which of these instruments does Justin not play?

a. Banjo   b. Trumpet   c. Piano

9. Justin's middle name is:

a. Drew   b. Edward   c. Andrew

10. The Biebs' concert at Madison Square Garden sold out in:

a. 22 minutes   b. 22 hours   c. 22 days

11. Which of these stars shares JB's birthday?

a. Lady Gaga   b. Ke$ha   c. Selena Gomez

12. One day, Justin would like to be:

a. An architect   b. A drama teacher   c. A radio talk show host

BORN TO BE SOMEBODY

At 17 years old, he's already super-successful. But what are Justin's plans for the future?

Stay in the Spotlight

Justin is loving his life on stage, on tour and in the spotlight. He's enjoying connecting with his fans, and has no plans to leave the music biz anytime soon. But music isn't the only thing Justin is interested in.

After making his own film, Justin would like to act in other roles. "I'm gonna start doing more movies — start getting more scripts and start finding some things that I really wanna do," he promises. He's even getting some help looking through scripts from Jaden and Willow Smith's dad, actor Will Smith.

Manager Scooter Braun also revealed that Justin is hoping to get to act alongside comic actor Will Ferrell.

The Next Michael Jackson?

It's no secret that Michael Jackson is someone who inspired Justin's music and dance style, and Justin and his team think that he could be the next MJ.

"Michael was so amazing. He worked so hard and knew how to manage his career. He's someone I look up to," Justin reveals.

Smart Move!

Justin isn't just a brilliant singer and dancer, he's also quite good at his studies. With nearly perfect grades, Justin hopes that he will be able to use his talents off-stage by attending university. Justin says, "I always travel with a private tutor who I have five three-hour sessions a week with. I want to finish high school and also college and then evolve wherever my music takes me."

Up!

No matter what happens in the future, one thing is for sure, Justin Bieber is only getting started in his successful journey. And he knows he couldn't have made it this far without his family, friends, fans and his dreams. "Follow your dreams," he says. "You can do anything you set your mind to." There's no stopping this star as he shoots to the top!

ALL THE ANSWERS

Never Say ... (pages 12–13)

1. Justin Bieber 2. Miranda Cosgrove 3. Justin Bieber 4. Justin Bieber 5. Sean Kingston 6. Taylor Swift 7. Katy Perry 8. Justin Bieber 9. Ellen DeGeneres 10. Justin Bieber

My Words (page 18)

Z	Y	G	O	S	O	S	B	F	G	J	Y	U	D	P
E	M	C	F	E	T	E	E	M	J	É	S	S	B	L
U	M	C	I	Q	Y	R	L	L	Q	L	J	M	Y	F
S	A	G	Y	O	S	T	A	P	E	O	X	I	B	H
A	R	P	N	E	J	J	E	T	Y	N	E	L	A	C
T	G	C	D	Z	N	H	L	G	F	G	A	E	E	O
H	É	R	E	T	T	I	W	T	A	Q	I	N	J	O
Z	C	G	F	É	H	O	Q	B	L	Z	R	P	C	W
Q	S	D	Z	O	I	O	H	S	L	P	R	D	I	Q
L	Q	H	V	B	N	N	O	X	C	A	Z	J	W	V
D	O	P	Z	X	P	H	N	N	Y	O	K	I	H	Y
F	B	W	B	Q	Q	T	U	F	P	B	O	R	W	D
Z	H	Z	J	R	E	L	L	I	R	H	T	T	É	M
I	U	T	L	Q	I	W	F	F	O	H	T	E	M
Q	T	L	J	C	G	P	H	M	Q	Y	X	U	O	R

Guess Who! (page 34)

1. False: actress Jessica Biel asked for $5,000; Justin hoped to raise $10,000 — and he did!

2. True: Justin Bieber and Ozzy Osbourne auctioned off the space suits they wore in a TV commercial in 2011. The money they raised went to a cancer charity.

3. True: Justin donated the money to the Community Foundation of Middle Tennessee's Nashville Flood Fund.

4. False: Oprah Winfrey signed the bone.

5. False: singer Bono helped to start this organization.

6. True.

7. False: author J. K. Rowling handwrote a history of one of the Harry Potter characters to raise money for Book Aid International.

8. True.

9. True.

10. False: Miley Cyrus donated a bag that she decorated.

The Ultimate Fan Quiz
(pages 56–57)

1. b — Spaghetti bolognese 2. a — *My World Tour* 3. c — Gwen Stefani 4. b — YouTube 5. a — Auckland, New Zealand 6. c — Scooter Braun 7. c — 2 8. a — Banjo 9. a — Drew 10. a — 22 minutes 11. b — Ke$ha 12. a — An architect